Up and L. . . . .

Written by Chris Lutrario
Illustrated by Scoular Anderson

Collins *Educational*
An imprint of HarperCollins *Publishers*

Up went the cat.

Up went the dog.

Up went the sheep.

Down came the cat.

Down came the dog.

Down came the sheep.